The Empty Form Goes All the Way to Heaven

The Empty Form

Goes All the Way

to Heaven

Brian Teare

Nightboat Books
New York

ISBN: 978-1-64362-159-3

Cover art and design by Kit Schluter
Design and typesetting by Janet Holmes and Kit Schluter
Typeset in Apollo and TitlingGothicGB

Cataloging-in-publication is available from the Library of Congress

Nightboat Books
New York
www.nightboat.org

for Jean Valentine

Contents

Preface

I.

There are an infinite number of different kinds of happiness.   18

And to think I am small and the work is small.   19

I am going to work in order to see myself and free myself.   20

Look between the rain. The drops are insular.   21

coloured pencil, graphite, and ink on paper, nine by nine inches   22

II.

white pencil on etching and aquatint proof, twelve and a quarter by twelve and a quarter inches   25

We are not the instruments of fate nor are we the pawns of fate we are the material of fate.   26

One must see the ideal in one's own mind. It is like the memory of perfection.   27

I lay down my gaze as one lays down one's weapons.   28

I give up facts entirely.   29

Going on where hope and desire have been left behind is a discipline.   31

I want to repeat: there are no valid thoughts about art.   32

It is hard to realize at the time of helplessness that that is the time to be awake and aware.   33

Perceiving *is the same as* receiving *and it is the same as* responding.   36

That is enough for death, now for real life.   37

We think that at last our feet are on the right path and we will not falter or fail.   39

Defeated, *you will perhaps go a little bit further.*   40

Preface

Agnes Martin (1912-2004) was an abstract expressionist painter. After two decades of dissatisfaction with her work, Martin found her signature vocabulary around 1960: the grid, the horizontal line, the tension between mathematical precision and hand application. These first mature works—as delicate and subtle as they are formal and even austere—were often mistaken for minimalism. "The grid's mythic power is that it makes us able to think we are dealing with materialism," critic Rosalind Krauss writes, "while at the same time it provides us with a release into belief." But Martin's investment in the grid is resolutely metaphysical. "One day when I was waiting for an inspiration, I was thinking of innocence, and a grid came into my mind," she tells documentarian Mary Lance, "and I painted the grid, six by six feet, and it looked like innocence."

Though Martin's mature work began in lower Manhattan, where she lived from 1957 until 1967, she is largely associated with the landscape of rural New Mexico. It was there, where she settled during the seven-year hiatus from painting that followed her exodus from New York, she began writing the texts that would accompany her first major retrospective, at the Institute for Contemporary Art (ICA) in Philadelphia in 1973. These texts, clearly inflected by her readings in Buddhism, mix the forms of wisdom literature and advice to artists in an idiom on the one hand dogmatic and prescriptive, and on the other lofty and idealistic. These and later writings draw deeply upon her core beliefs in inspiration, perfection, Classicism, solitude, freedom, happiness, non-attachment, humility, and a withdrawal from the sociopolitical. "We seem to be winning or losing/but in reality there is no losing," she writes at the close of "The Untroubled Mind," "The wiggle of a worm is as important as the assassination of a president."

Martin insisted that her paintings recorded her emotions, but she rarely allowed her private life to become public record. Just prior to the ICA retrospective, critic and filmmaker Lizzie Borden traveled to New Mexico to interview Martin for *Art Forum*. "She revealed so much to me about her life that I'll never be able to print," Borden writes Suzanne Delahanty, then director of the ICA, "I had to minimize on information, and as you know, she hates the idea of the 'artist' being talked about." After moving to New Mexico, where she lived alone until her death, Martin was largely a recluse, but her luminous work, her growing fame, her commitment to the artist's life, and her sage-like habit of coining quotable aphorisms inspired young artists, writers, and curators like Borden, Jill Johnston, and Douglas Crimp, among others, to seek her out.

When in 2009 I began writing the poems in this book, I knew nothing about Agnes Martin. Early during the onset of a chronic illness, I opened her *Writings* and found "The Untroubled Mind" to be a comfort. But as the illness deepened I began to "seek her out" when I could through research in museums, libraries, and archives. These poems set my life in relation to my long encounter with her painting, drawing, writing, and the metaphysics she argued was implicit in them. Those who were compelled to visit Martin in New Mexico often felt they did not wish to disappoint her by falling short of the ideals she and her art embodied with admirable and rigorous purity. Alone with her work for many years, I felt the same way until I didn't.

watercolor and graphite on paper, fifteen by fifteen inches

::   a color field   a sort of tea-colored leakage   a headache   ::

::   the texture of paper bag and over it a grid in graphite fitted   ::

::   to a grid of white pencil   an almost subliminal flickering   ::

::   where my body first enters the picture   the inscription   ::

::   of conflicting readings   the work's surface touched by   ::

::   the brush all pooled color and puckered grain   a form   ::

::   narrowed down to its final iteration   internally organized   ::

::   and complete because of its tensions   I am speaking   ::

::   of illness and the critical situation it reveals   as my own   ::

::   embodied gaze   the loom upon which materiality turns   ::

::   pictorial its likeness to fabric heightened by fibers swollen   ::

::   torqued by tint   caught in its operations   I insert a knot   ::

::   between the warp and weft of the observed surface words   ::

::   to stop the work of the lyric   to stop the mortal thought   ::

There are two endless directions. In and out.

afternoon

cloud cover
alters symmetry's

brief virtue

                                          illness posits
trellis and shadow
classic image

                                          its question
                                          will mind or body
two late T'ang dishes

                                          be the first
one flowering
one empty

                                          fugitive clarity
                                          of a day's gray

                                          scale study

Defeated you will stand at the door of your house and welcome the unknown.

chronic nausea
chronic non

narrative even
the public health

                    eventually the surface gets interesting

clinic's waiting
room more

                    affect   *to wait* the purling of signature

gestural than
temporal

                    events   like the calm after vomiting

                    the sum of a knitter's dropped stitches

                          barren orchid
a continual doing undone   in which   slumped glossy

                          monthlies   stained
the assembled material dissembles   public fabric

                          patient number
without voice   I mean illness has none   0 1 7 1 9 0 6 7

                          uninsured
I speak on behalf of what expels me   no other place

                          to go   I had
                          to bring my body

Then I painted the two rectangles.

western window
eastern window
sickbed between

illness shares
its few virtues   with art   pain
                               as anomalous
                               as imagination

in not being "of"
or "for" anything

                               even language
                               lacks the quality
                               of their solitude

pure process
like art   illness is

                               mostly the mystery
                               of why one window
                               opens slowly

why one window
remains locked

With these rectangles I didn't know at the time exactly why.

old tin tub

soapy water
tilts over

its rim   hits
nice image   linoleum

for nausea   how small
washing hot

                                          my body
one end   has become
to the other
             I remember   again

             my mother
             poured warm

             water over

There is the work in our minds, the work in our hands, and the work as a result.

not yet diagnosed   without a language for it   ill of body or mind

ill of body *and* mind   a narrative I watch   the doctor assemble

a diagnostic sentence   prescription a script   clinic a proscenium

I return to as audience

to watch my body
                                                             blue square framed in white
symptoms a form   on cool bathroom linoleum
                                                             smallest hour of symptom
of prosthesis   the sharp pure urge to puke
                                                             an argument about unlikeness
performed to help me   my body fits to itself roughly
                                                             a blade chafing its sheath
to know my part

This poem, like the paintings, is not really about nature.

a summer forest
thrust through
the poem starts

when I lie down   I mean firs
I've been felled   surround
                                                   the russet floor
                    what good
                    will it do to desire
                    what will do no good   my lover's
      one season's   beard   his kiss
      resilient knit
      of twigs   to fall

      ill is this   field unprepared
      long drought   for winter rain
                                   the first downpour

                                   will wash topsoil off
                                   in rich folds of silt

If you don't like chaos you're a classicist.

from my bed's edge
I take a step
forward   everywhere

what is the ideal
state of illness

this dualist
feeling of dispersal   does it want
concentrating   to attain anything

warmth   thought
at root transparent

consciousness
diminished then
distance lingers

my whole body
in the ten directions

If you like it you're a romantic.

like *luck* lilts   first toward *lurk*
lack follows   as far as symptom

ill I attempt
    a long time
to experience
    diagnosis

but pain is more
    the way fire is

an animal
    in its several colors
so at home

If there is a bare spot on the ground the best possible weed for
that environment will grow.

public health clinic
squeaky cheap chair

I open the book
and Lao Tzu says   an old Christian word
                                    patient at root means

knowing how to
endure is wisdom   *to suffer* its definition
                                    both longsuffering

                                    and one undergoing
                                    medical treatment

                                    study to be patient
                                    in suffering counsels

Jesse the phlebotomist
needs only two sticks   *De Imitatione Christi*

then the five vials
one by one grow warm

                                                    I leave the clinic dizzy
an eye's run of rhymes   in the crook of my arm
ruby beauty rutilant

                                                    gauze and two band-aids
                                                    the book of wisdom

reading Agnes Martin
on the bus I think
about her "perfection"
for about four blocks
until I begin to hate it

a word changes as it enters a new discourse
freed from received ideas and responsibilities
stripped to its core it's made "perfect"
but a word might choose to change itself

in the drawings I love
she leaves evidence
of process fraying
the grid's edge
like leftover math

outside the realm of perspective
a line that constructs a system
continually escapes perfection
a kind of found quality persisting

a word might choose its medium

her forms suggest
a counter-rhetoric
dots of color or
the hand-drawn
incidental
serves as a frame

graphite over a light acrylic wash
emptiness as an outer limit or
graffiti scratched into the bus window
existence makes a thing useful
nonexistence makes it work
the impossible patterns a life

We cannot understand everything that happens to everyone.

days of headache
flushed hot skin

my mind a loose
weave stained by
thoughts it's lost

illness keeps
a little calendar

the look of water
color on cotton

so few memories
I return to these
colors as evidence

I'm writing it
by natural light

Not to know, but to go on.

white underpainting
floats up through   milky as wringing
darker colors it carries   just-washed glue
                           brushes over the sink

  as water floats paper
  before saturation   waiting is the color
  reveals its inks   of what draws nearer
                           without touching

The writing fills the space as drawing would.

                                    hours without
                                    words   I can't

                                    form   space
can't hold any   contour   my body
thing interior

never empties
of what it has

to do   ache   wavers in the tin

                                    tub where also I
                                    bobbed for apples

                                    until my face hurt

and hunger can't urge me   a child
sitting in snow   to open my mouth

This developing awareness I will also call "the work." It is a most important part of the work.

I look at paintings

Agnes Martin made

and I wonder about

the grid as endgame

not a spiritual practice

but the mind's limit

I know she believed

art is better hungry

before I became ill

I could eat without fear

my lover could enter me

and I desired nothing else

There are an infinite number of different kinds of happiness.

the grain of the page softened

by cotton   the hand-drawn
line like the poetic line implies

a law of perspective   a body   somehow   walking to the hospital
a strangely spacious framework   dim daylight   I stop to watch sunrise
                                         buildings   fat finches sit by the ER
in which to consider the mortal   higher up   in stripped twig-work
                                         shading off   late hawthorn berries
                                         into fog   frayed red gray feathers

And to think I am small and the work is small.

/

/

consciousness is spatial
/ a really empty painting

/

white hospital bed
/ before I get into it

/

thought takes shape
/ <u>where is this headed</u>

/

sheet blanket sheet
/ intravenous shiver

/

the picture fills up
/ dressed for a visit

/

soft graphite lines
/ a gown worn backwards

/

soft graphite lines
/ a gown worn forwards

/

/

I am going to work in order to see myself and free myself.

ass exposed again   a certain detachment

during the probe   I keep bending over
                              now I want to write about all the time I've spent
meanwhile thinking   doctors can help
                              waiting at the edge of the examination table
though most often they tell me they can't
                              afraid I'm going to tear the stiff hygienic paper
uninsured   I've run out of available tests
                              now I want to write about the fact I can't choose
the official diagnosis   it's all in my head
                              what else I'll lose by being ill   the prognosis

                              my future project   to learn to think with pain

Look between the rain. The drops are insular.

to pass through

a downpour
and to stay dry I have to choose
                    the right image

that's emptiness
                    to center between

                    rest and *pain*
                    as between two

                    teeth on a gear
I'll hollow out

                    for my mind to lock
like a gourd   on the thought
to hold water

the point is

to pour out
caught by nothing

::   I look into my mind   as into one of Agnes Martin's grids   ::

::   a field of consciousness   tint and hue touch and pool   ::

::   a non-semantic ambience   thought after thought   ::

::   a pink ink wash   wrinkling the paper at its left edge   ::

::   three vertical lines in red pencil   what am I looking for   ::

::   the rest of the grid in graphite   the form is familiar   ::

::   but I don't feel at home   not even around the periphery   ::

::   in small mistakes   that exceed the grid's strict measures   ::

::   ink leaking into the margin   in the middle of my life   ::

::   I've become strange to myself   red accident at the edge   ::

::   I mean to be clear   I'm not lost   ::

::   a guide on each side to keep my hand level   a small series   ::

::   of dots to true the ruler   the frame as white as the time   ::

::   I spent under anesthesia   I lean my thinking against it   ::

white pencil on etching and aquatint proof, twelve and a quarter by
twelve and a quarter inches

the grid's a little calendar I put each minute into

an elongated box   grey with an *e*   the color

of the thinking preceding   a divisive brightness

the time before migraine   or the thin needles

the healer sinks in my head   to release its heat

let's put this minute between the need to vomit

and the history of metaphysics   my hot mind

cleared of its luminous fogs   I polish each line

of white pencil and think   being ill makes me

an object full of a process   hard to see at work

inside my body   the lyric might be a plastic art

after all   if my voice also takes place as a shape

arranged to stop the pain   when I pin the grid

with acupuncture needles   the page clicks shut

We are not the instruments of fate nor are we the pawns of fate we are the material of fate.

I leave each doctor's appointment ashamed to be ill

                    the philosopher argues the verbal expression of pain

undiagnosed my body so illegible no one can read it

                    replaces pain without offering a description of it

I don't yet know the only thing doctors can tell me

                    the sensation of pain helplessly separate from language

the true human body is just the true human body

                    I turn toward this little apostrophe in the dark of me

it goes under anesthesia and it wakes up the same

                    I listen to it as if pain were a saying I could transcribe

its gut lit up by the camera gives nothing away

                    there's no language for it and my work doesn't describe it

                    I've had to find a form able to do what I mean

                    I mean I've had to fashion a form that *pains*

One must see the ideal in one's own mind. It is like the memory of perfection.

the doctors treat my body
only as the site of disorder
the way it's easy to think
meaning arises from words
as though a body or lyric
doesn't begin outside itself

in pain I need help
I open the book
Agnes wrote to say
beauty is unattached
a clear mind sees it

embedded in and open to
weather and culture alike
no system a single entity

the whole point is
when I finally give up
I won't get anything
I must suffer first
to be freed from it

no body a closed border
imbalance enters my body
the lyric a part of its pattern

I lay down my gaze as one lays down one's weapons.

'

the ideal hurts   I can't desire
I can't experience   health without
being ill   wanting my "old self" back

I DON'T KNOW
HOW TO READ THIS

wandering away   not thinking   not planning
giving up everything   not striving or caring
not me anymore   is a discipline

someone's saying
always in voiceover

then I draw a picture of   I draw a picture
the lyric   I draw it   of the lyric   I draw it
so I can point to it   so I can correct it

WHEN I GIVE UP
I FEEL A LOT BETTER

I give up facts entirely.

but not before
each needle

the healer sets
in my flesh

is a fact
I feel

network lit
point to point

by memory
January's

homeward
path lined by

snapped
birch-backs

arched above
drifts holding

crowns down
"weak trees

can't bend"
my neighbor said

years ago
I wake up

my head's hot
wood element

in the healer's
silver hands

Going on where hope and desire have been left behind is a discipline.

in pain   I don't experience pain as repetition

though I've knelt into nausea this way before

and bent   reminiscent of prayer or surrender

like looking again at Agnes's painting *The Beach*

the texture of a tissue protecting an engraving

pain touches the mind with a similar distance

entirely prepositional   dependent on proximity

an order bordering on the look of a thing

seen by a dreamer   my sense of self returns

without illness   a casual traveler   book in hand

glare flares from the page struck by sunlight

I'm a patient of clinics and a writer of lyrics
at the last doctor's appointment I can afford

wearing a thin cotton gown paid for by taxes
I think about the lyric   I'm really thinking

in late late capitalism's miniature exam room
of faith   I was taught to be a believer

medical truth is entirely reliant upon money
in the power of poets and doctors   TRUTH

lyric truth has one legible and one illegible body
sitting in the bare cold folding metal chair

one patient of the clinic and one writer of lyrics
the doctor really *is* saying IT'S ALL IN YOUR HEAD

—but there are no valid thoughts about art!

It is hard to realize at the time of helplessness that that is the time to be awake and aware.

a fiction
devoid of
anything real

first diagnosis   / you will
                                die young

second diagnosis   / you will die
                                young and
                                in great pain   a thought
                                                       keeps creating
                                                       the mind

third diagnosis   / you will die
                                eventually   claiming it
                                                       exists

meanwhile
the image is
as it does

         in her hands
         the healer takes
         my head

I lie down
somatic

an egg that
when cracked
won't crack

she helps thought
through heat

thick as wool felt
reach consciousness   it is sorrow   without form
                             to intuit thoughts   no tendons or bones

                             occurring elsewhere
                             as certain as sun
                             behind cloud-cover

                             and as lost to me   metaphor
pure motion !   needs the body

Perceiving is the same as *receiving* and it is the same as *responding*.

thought begins as small floral bowls   they hold greens   broccoli stalks

                                               chopped kale   against Chinese blue

                                               very dark   with a greenish tint

the way a silence falls to each side

of the knife's stroke   the colors rhyme

softly and I think *I'll miss this when I die*   this is how I enter appearances

That is enough for death, now for real life.

most days
a remove

           not *my* hand
           a hand holds

between me
and real life

           the book that
           just yesterday

not people
not things

           I read closely
           so many days

just images
bus glass

           I say goodbye
           to my mind

glare

           dog-eared page

good days

                                    it feels like
                                    simile can't

return to

                                    make it feel
                                    I stood once

the page

                                    on the side
                                    of the highway

and turn

                                    in Wyoming
                                    sky so close

its corner up

                                    curved away

We think that at last our feet are on the right path and we will not falter or fail.

sometimes I still feel
very *why me* about it

very Christian I mean
I'm convinced   for weeks returning
                                                           to one book as if

I believe suffering
interpreted correctly   to make a medicine
                                                           of its vocabulary

could be *really useful*
                                                           while I wait I read
                                                           as if a certain diction

                                    at first   could help only if
in *On Light* I read   it seemed   I've made it a charm
matter cannot be

                                    awful   through continual use
emptied of form   to be ill
form is light itself

                                    without
                                    purpose

                                    now
                                    I have *lumen*

                                    enough
                                    to have

                                    nothing
                                    and that

Defeated, you will perhaps go a little bit further.

I wake to headache
as to the phrase
ALWAYS ALREADY

stress unstress
unstress stress
unstress mind

meanwhile caught
on the desire to see   what I have most of
itself without need   is lack

of an illustrative image   so I build with it
                                        crow feathers

                                        saturated black
                                        as fuel coal

          between her hands   on the wet sidewalk
            the healer makes   a bird's worth
             my skull a page
                                        scattered
           scored with folds
          to teach it to open
           thinking's screen

                a paper window
                twilight outside
                pictorial the pond

                 beneath the pines
                 collects signatures
                  for the rain

This developing awareness I will also call "the work." It is a most important part of the work.

I work on another poem

with a ruler and pencil

compulsory repetition

helpless entrapment

or meditative lyric

iterated constantly?

satisfaction's impossible

but I remember how

I could open my mouth

I could be nourished

until illness entered me

more deeply than health

We seem to be winning and losing, but there is no losing.

after World War II

          unable to eat   unbidden the image

food was scarce   often returns

          unable to write

in East Germany

           unable to read   usually more

my friend tells me   as color   ivory

            I think

her grandmother

             of the story   interior flecked

gently used the tip   red   sometimes

             she told me

of her right forefinger

              as a parable   more as sound

to clean each eggshell   her forefinger

                                      careful   scrapes

tip against paper

With a soft attitude, you receive more.

a question of mind

what begins there   tongue and pulses
what ends there   a question of reading

I keep thinking it
a site of arrival

                           I believe if I'm quiet what's wrong will be legible
it might not be   or the healer can say I've improved

I hold the plate
over the garbage

                           I tell myself I was
and scrape it   once without pain
once with a knife

                           perhaps I was not yet conscious of it
                           the way a wire kept the rose upright in bloom

                           I couldn't tell
                           until I held it

We cannot even imagine how to be humble.

/

dear poem I give up
trying to tell the story \ difficult to guard and hard to restrain

/

because I turned God
inside-out like a sock \ It is good to tame the mind

/

now I sit on a cushion
void I bend one way \ Wandering far and alone, intangible

/

toward alignment
void I bend the other \ the one who has let go of gain and loss

/

toward fatigue
at the bus stop \ this body cast away, without consciousness

/

I bend over the curb
nauseous "Nice ass" \ A tamed mind gives rise to ease

/

someone says

I'm not trying to describe anything. I'm looking for the perfect space.

wisdom has said
we have a body
we have disaster
rectangle and square   to write is to draw
a thinking couple   between the mark
                              and its support
illness narrows   the soft grid a size
the visual field   I can walk into
but can't close it
sufficient difference   for all its regularity
establishes an opening   a dream of graphite
                                   I almost remember
                                   the root of light
                                   heavy in my hand

Somebody's got to sit down and really want it.

everybody is born   after eating lunch
in the same condition   I feel so sleepy

a little figure with a sword   I have this mind
I thought I was going   from present to future

to cut my way through life   no joy   no sorrow
victory after victory   I was sure   this body steadfast

I was going to do it   one thousand three hundred nights

pencil on aquatint ground, twelve and a half by twelve inches

::   this afternoon the rain begins   to make a place for the pictorial   ::

::   the page a wash of nausea   fogged and oddly shiny, silver-black   ::

::   everyone leaving the building pausing   saying   oh, it's a *hot* rain   ::

::   dissolving powdery ground   the texture left on the etching plate   ::

::   is true   but I worry about the long sharp pain in my side   ::

::   and later a ruler   laid over the atmosphere of cognitive distress   ::

::   clicks open   my spine the black stem of an elegant umbrella   ::

::   my ribs curve up into a bell   whose wide mouth holds no tongue   ::

::   as if to incise the scumble with lines   would turn it toward order   ::

::   I take a pencil   and draw forth the scaffold on which I stand over   ::

::   the storm   each street rings with it   steaming in the heat   ::

::   each line an ashen azimuth   in the visual field bordered by white   ::

::   made whiter by proximity   the image of illness relentlessly total   ::

::   the way from indoors the sound of rain is both figure and ground   ::

watercolor, ink and gouache on paper, nine and a quarter by nine
and a quarter inches

//   paper responds to water by curling   suffering   \\

\\   an essential volatility in the medium   restraint   //

//   is beneficial   the teacher Buddha repeats   restraint   \\

\\   of the body is beneficial   I can see the touch   //

//   of Agnes's brush   paper's grain opened up to color   \\

\\   the way I imagine pain enters my body   a process   //

//   that alters the fate of each fiber   felted together   \\

\\   in the same direction   when the nausea arrives   //

//   I close my eyes   I look into the black ink grid   \\

\\   laid over the pool of fluctuating blue   perfectly   //

//   composed   I think though I try for detachment   \\

\\   I achieve a form of sublimated rage   each flat line   //

//   flattened by hand   until language is restrained   \\

\\   all around   the practitioner released from pain   //

When pride in some form is lost, we feel very different.

illness means a lot less
self which isn't so bad

hard to say what else
persists chronically

migrainous nauseous
abdominal cramping

the healer uses needles
to calm like revision

might make the poem
less stupid as the body

is likely to throw up
re: ultimate authority

what kind of body
forgets how to eat

hot with hatred
a minor literature

I needle each word
until it bleeds

I painted a painting called *This Rain*.

why return again to
a limited vocabulary   it's the inexhaustible
                          nature of limitation

the way symptoms
recur during a day   using what few words
                          I'm allowed to keep

my body becomes
a repeated thought   I try to describe rain
                          for the pain of it

my mind returns
to the meal I can't eat   I try to describe rain
                           a repcatcd thought

if I eat I won't sleep
for the pain of it   the way we experience
                          a picture makes it real

I return again to my
limited vocabulary   it's the inexhaustible
                          symptom during a day

I try to describe the meal
I can't eat I won't sleep while I think of it
                           a picture makes it real

The process called destiny in which we are the material to be dissolved.

on camera the teacher Agnes

gessoes the canvas   I like
                              to lie my mind down beneath each brushstroke
to watch linen turn thick white
                              unrolling neatly from the brush a clean bandage
I want to cut the picture down
                              it doesn't look hard   but it's really difficult
I mute the sound   the frame

empties itself of literal image

                                        the cheapest available material
                beneath many layers of giving up
                                        the critic claims   is the artist's body
        I found a therapeutic form of impasse
                                        I like to think it supports the poem
        illness speaking itself as symptom
                                        the way linen supports the painting

                                        if to imagine a larger form is to heal

                                        how wide would four blue bands be

Any mistake in the scale and it doesn't work out. It's pretty hard because it's such a small picture.

the problem with illness
is I think there might be   too much heat
a way to be ill that would   in the spleen
free me from suffering   general fatigue
the way correctly placed   foggy vision
needles calm symptoms   stomach spasms

during headache's iterations   in the old medical textbook
I begin to miss visual images   each pressure point turns
though lyric is a woven grid   metaphorical
hard stresses threading weft   thought shelter
through the warp of stacked
lines the last stanza finished   labor palace
I put my ear to its little box

                                     dwelling bone

                                     broken bowl

As grass that is hard to grasp cuts the hand itself.

I have no memory   for a long time
            people are just like the grass
for a long time   I lie on my back

feeling otherwise   loving questions

all events take place   because I think

in the present tense   I have no answers
            the teacher Agnes says
I lie on my back   I have no choice

pain is this verb   I have to live this life

whose gist I feel   as I know it to be

beneath my ribs   led by mind
        a blade of grass doesn't amount to much
a statement   formed by mind

phrased as a question   that is also my body

What you do is get rid of everything.

I don't want to be a prisoner   let your body be your teacher
                    even if you are a prisoner
I don't want to be defeated   the healer says   follow it
                    the teacher Buddha says
I want to be at rest in matter   your body knows what to do
                    when you rise and stand up
I want to fit into my body   the idea moves me   I love
                    you are only that standing up
the way the femur's head sits   the healer   she is wrong
                    but illness stands up with me
in its slick pelvic socket   I can't keep anything down
                    I love the teacher Buddha
then the illness worsens   I vomit and weep until empty
                    he is wrong   I give up

                    I get rid of everything

If we are completely without direction our minds will tell us the next step to take.

for five years I wait for pain
to make meaning of my life

in the emergency room light tilts sidewise on the floor tiled in a grid

but I am only remembering
promises made in childhood

white the color of waiting the correlative to long duration without event

Book I of *De Imitatione Christi* says
it is good for man to suffer

the washed cotton of hospital gowns soft as the cognitive fog of illness

the adversity of earthly life
accustomed to seeing illness

vaguely interested in emergency as a heightened mode of interpretation

from the outside as a parable
for five years I write poems

at last the needle hits the vein the sudden blush of blood in the test tube

whether I can walk or not
I give my own life the shape

      each sense a membrane vulnerable to the way the nurse sharply says *breathe*

lent to it only by watching
myself believe in the benefit

      the white of ice water in a Styrofoam cup and a pill in a pleated paper cup

of a suffering so absolute
we should never think it

      the mind's response to line and color the same as its response to sounds

necessary in any distress
to have recourse to human

      until event punctures duration and a sense of self rushes into the visual field

consolations but I who am
watching never believed it

      I am cold and afraid and alone and I have to piss but I've gotten too sick to walk

and I who write this now
no longer believe it is good

       on the gurney in the hallway I begin to believe my response to emergency

I no longer believe it is bad
I only believe it is suffering

       reveals the metaphysical grammar I will employ for the rest of my life

and it means nothing at all

When I cover the square surface with rectangles, it destroys its power.

I said I dreamt another grid   I meant I slept upon a fishhook

the mark of human meaning   and drew all those rectangles

my body was just like them   a little bit off the square

I said I found the look of order   a comfort in discomfort

I meant you can't get away   from what you have to do

off the path of the true life   the mind says *Yes* and *No*

making a sort of contradiction   that's the way to freedom

This developing awareness I will also call "the work." It is a most important part of the work.

I look at paintings

        I work on another poem

the teacher Agnes made

        with a ruler and pencil

and I wonder about

        compulsory repetition

the grid as endgame

        helpless entrapment

not a spiritual practice

        or meditative lyric

but the mind's limit

        iterated constantly

I know she believed

        satisfaction impossible

art is better hungry

        but I remember how

before I became ill

        I could open my mouth

I could eat without fear

        I could be nourished

my lover could enter me

                    until illness entered me

and I desired nothing else

                    more deeply than health

People that look out with their backs to the world represent something that isn't possible in this world.

|| too ill to leave home   I think of the sentence ||

Agnes is famous for   and admit I don't know

what it means   to turn your back to the world

and paint against it   all its antagonistic

and contesting parts   I know she chose the grid

for its purity   its signature without ego   I know

too she chose to leave   in each line evidence

of her hand in the process of drawing   I think

about turning my back to the world and writing

but when I turn inward and look   I understand

the assemblage from first to last   I am the way

her hand everywhere   fastens the grid

to itself   with a line   a pencil   body   mind

there's nowhere the world doesn't hold me here

As grass that is hard to grasp cuts the hand itself.

for a long time   I lie on my back
                        in the visual field
I lie on my back   and think I can

loving questions   think my way

because I think   through pain
                        wind is a great comfort
I have no answers   as if I knew

I have no choice   no difference

I have to live life   between pain
                        the teacher Agnes says
as I know it to be   and thinking

led by mind   looking always

formed by mind   for safe passage
                        religion is about this grass
that is also my body   between them

wretched thou art
wherever thou art

> I sit and work on a line and lean into the pain my mind continues
> trying to think and all I come up with is a texture without ideas

and to whatever
thou turnest —

> the body I have is the body I once had but they could not differ more
> the teacher Agnes says abstract form holds meaning beyond words

I turn the pages
of the old book

> the way certain feelings come to us with no discernible worldly cause
> the teacher Buddha says the practitioner agitated by thoughts

I have not held
since childhood

> makes stronger their bondage to suffering and the sting of becoming
> during the time illness makes me feel most tied to the material world

its binding broken
its brittle paper

> I sit in meditation and sunlight from the window calms my nausea
> since the emergency I feel such sharp tenderness toward common objects

its dog-eared corners
torn at the folds —

       sort of attached to the white wall white door white dust on the wood floor
       mostly pain is an endless present tense without depth or discernible shape

miserable are all
who have not

       an image or memory lends it a passing contour or a sort of border
       the white door open against the white wall snuffs headache's first flare

a sense of present
life's corruption

       I remember a man patiently crying as doctors drained his infected wound
       lying on the gurney in my hospital gown we suffered from having been being

but much more
miserable are those

       adjacent and precarious the way a practitioner sits alone on a cushion
       resting alone unwearied alone taming himself yet I was no longer alone

in love with it —

I pretend I was looking at the blank page.

I look into my mind and see nothing   my immediate effort   as in all arts
all opposites dead to the world   is form   yet technique is a hazard

metaphor allows   my own illness
    my body to be both   the tool I use
language and nest   with much exertion
   less weaving   I press and knead
than *condensation*   the materials
                                                              beaten   blended
                                                                  welded together

the meaning of suffering hidden from me   perhaps now I can really enjoy writing

Horizontal lines for forty years.

it doesn't matter where I work

the environment has no impact

like many of her later paintings

or this life   I mean   on earth

full of sweet sentimental color

it took me twenty years to paint

and I didn't sell   but finally

the grid   it was what I wanted

no longer a friend, master, slave

no hint of any cause in this world

I watch the documentary again

though the teacher repeats herself

because I don't paint nature

too smooth in its execution

I've grown tired of her rhetoric

what I wanted   I didn't show

I know I need something she offers

but I no longer know what it is

completely abstract   absolutely

Agnes is my teacher until she isn't

Form is created as you look at it and it sinks away as you look at it.

```
                                        \
                                         \
        it's hard to get comfortable      \      when I leave the teacher
        nausea lodges its one thought       \    tells me she is hesitant
        in my gut     but I sit with it      \    about friendship
        like I would a difficult friend      \
```

don't be fond of me

```
        hard to let go     language       /
        to admit at last it's nothing      /     let's not be friends
        and multiplies that nothing        /     let's be companions
        endless    a field     drifting    /     of the open road
                                           /
                                          /
```

I am nothing absolutely. There is this other thing going on.

at the museum
I see *Night Sea*

blue-green grid
framed in goldleaf

the visual field
water's tension

I see the poem is
partial knowledge

an excerpt implying
more than it makes

overt   it leaves
itself unfinished

at the point just
prior to spillage

the grid essentially
kintsugi   beauty

cleaving to injury
soldered in gold

at its several edges
where the eye seeks

a way toward closure
that is not symmetry

form empties itself
on its way to heaven

When you come to the end of all ideas you will still have no
definitive knowledge on the subject.

and then I remember   I thought I *fell* ill

as though health   were a kind of eden

full of needles   I'm happy to find rest

on my back for an hour   looking west

out the window   her last painting

bands of dark and light grey   acrylic

on linen   the darker bands textured

uneven   weather she passed through

on her way somewhere else   suffering

is like that too   five horizontal lines

drawn in graphite grounding the canvas

it's hard not to see clouds when looking

at clouds   untitled like everything else

it took a long time   to arrive at being ill

without falling   I'm happy   I really like

this painting   there's no salvation in it

Dedications

I

watercolor and graphite on paper, fifteen by fifteen inches // Martha Ronk
If there is a bare spot on the ground . . . // Kerri Webster
We cannot understand everything that happens to everyone. // Sally Keith
There are an infinite number of different kinds of happiness. // Stephen Motika
And to think I am small and the work is small. // Lisa Russ Spaar
coloured pencil, graphite, and ink on paper, nine by nine inches // Gillian Conoley

II

white pencil on etching and aquatint proof . . . // Susan M. Schultz
We are not the instruments of fate nor are we the pawns of fate . . . // Alec Finlay
I give up facts entirely. // Marintha Tewksbury
Going on where hope and desire have been left behind is a discipline. // Carol Snow
I want to repeat: there are no valid thoughts about art. // Allison Cobb
We seem to be winning and losing, but there is no losing. // Antje Hofmeister
Defeated, you will perhaps go a little bit further. // Norma Cole
We cannot even imagine how to be humble. // Hoa Nguyen
I'm not trying to describe anything. I'm looking for the perfect space. // Kathleen Fraser

III

watercolor, ink and gouache on paper . . . // Catie Rosemurgy
The process called destiny in which we are the material . . . // Eleni Stecopolous
People that look out with their backs to the world represent something . . . // Rick Barot
I am nothing absolutely. There is this other thing going on. // Frances Richard
When you come to the end of all ideas you . . . // CAConrad

The Extent to Which the Body Becomes Thinkable:
Declan Gould Interviews Brian Teare

When Brian and I sat down under the fluorescent lights of a grimy, mostly-empty Buffalo subway car in the winter of 2016, I did not have the faintest idea we were about to begin a conversation that would continue intermittently for over five years. Brian was in town to give a reading as part of the University at Buffalo Poetics Plus series, and he had arrived a day early to visit the Poetry Collection. So together, we made the trek up to campus, him to spend some time with the Robert Duncan collection and me to teach my composition class. Our conversations about Brian's remarkable book, *The Empty Form Goes All the Way to Heaven* (first published by Ahsahta Press in 2015), ended up taking on a life of their own, and originally appeared in *Denver Quarterly* in 2018. We have expanded the original interview for the reissue of the book, using the final question from 2017 as a segue into three new questions, which Brian generously responded to in the spring of 2022.

As Brian states in the interview, he began writing *The Empty Form* in the summer of 2009 and completed the manuscript in the winter of 2015. During this period, Brian lived with a severe, undiagnosed illness and chronic pain. Importantly, the five plus years that Brian spent writing this text also overlapped with the publication of *Beauty Is A Verb: The New Disability Poetry* and with the work of the Nonsite Collective, a loosely affiliated, interdisciplinary Bay Area collaborative that was active from 2007 to 2011 and included disability studies scholars and poets Michael Davidson, Amber DiPietra, Thom Donovan, Patrick Durgin, David Wolach, Susan Schweik, and Eleni Stecopoulos (among others).

The *Empty Form* can be read as an incisive depiction of the medical–industrial complex from a patient's perspective, and it can also be read as a critique of capitalism, especially of the ways that our economic system engenders an individualizing ethos that frames illness as a personal failing and cure as a moral imperative (this reading is especially salient when considered in the context of the Great Recession and the Occupy Movement, which both occurred during the same period that Brian was writing these poems). Other readings could focus on Brian's ekphrastic responses to Agnes Martin's writing and visual art, his meditations on Zen Buddhism, his examination of the Christian belief that suffering is a means of salvation, or his exploration of embodied experience. However, in this introduction, I argue that *The Empty Form* is first and foremost a work of experimental disability poetry.

In *Concerto for the Left Hand*, Michael Davidson views disability aesthetics as foregrounding "the extent to which the body becomes thinkable when its totality can no longer be taken for granted, when the social meanings attached to sensory and cognitive values cannot be assumed." Just as disability aesthetics defamiliarize embodied experiences that reveal the vulnerability, instability, and complexity of the bodymind, the poems in *The Empty Form* are the basis for Brian's process of learning how to write poetry while living with an undiagnosed chronic illness whose symptoms included nausea, vomiting, joint pain, headaches, mental fogginess, and severe digestion problems. He articulates the process of rethinking his body in relation to this illness in "I pretend I was looking at the blank page:"

metaphor allows
my body to be both
language and nest
less weaving
than condensation

the meaning of suffering hidden from me

In other words, his understanding of his body—which is developed through the writing of these poems—is mobile, and has the potential to shift depending on what the situation calls for.

Like disability aesthetics' invitation to rethink the body and question assumptions about disability versus normativity and illness versus health, experimental poetry questions and dismantles normativity as an aesthetic and sociopolitical ideal, opening up ways of thinking difference beyond the disabled versus normal binary. In light of this resonance, experimental disability poetry like *The Empty Form* is uniquely positioned to explore not only concepts of the normal (which have manifested historically as exclusion of, violence against, and discursive diminishment of those deemed abnormal or disabled, as scholars like Ellen Samuels and Lennard Davis have shown), but also how these concepts get reproduced through inherited aesthetic traditions. In contrast, *The Empty Form* offers representations of an interdependent bodymind constituted by social and material situations that change over time.

For example, by juxtaposing "chronic nausea" with "chronic non / / narrative," Brian suggests that there is a connection between recurring nausea and the persistent refusal or inability to turn one's experiences into a linear, stable, or conventionally coherent narrative. But the exact nature of this relationship is left open-ended, creating a sense of being suspended in a state of uncertainty that is supported by Brian's visual forms, which resist the assumption that a page should only be read left to right and top to bottom by instead utilizing the space of the page in ways that encourage the eye to travel in different directions.

The Empty Form offers readers an important and much-needed example of a poetics that interweaves an exploration of embodied experience with an investigation into how this experience can be enacted in and investigated through poetic form. This extraordinary collection surely has had and will continue to have a major influence on experimental disability poetry as a developing field, which is also currently being explored by (among others) Meg Day, Amber DiPietra, JJJJJerome Ellis, Denise Leto, Jordan Scott, Eleni Stecopoulos, David Wolach, and Adam Wolfond.

I have experienced firsthand how simultaneously dehumanizing and life-changing, opaque and illuminating the diagnosis process can be. Like most people, I have also tried to support loved ones who live with illness and disability, and I have seen their struggles exacerbated by the harmful ways that Western culture—from our educational and legal institutions to our medical and capitalist systems—teach us to think and feel about incapacity, pain, embodied difference, in(ter)dependence, and the fluidness of our bodyminds. Like Audre Lorde's *Cancer Journals* and Eli Clare's *Brilliant Imperfection*, *The Empty Form* serves as an example of how to resist this miseducation while also using the knowledge gained from lived experience to chart a new path. As Brian says, entering an unfamiliar poetic form can cause frustration and pain, but it is also an invitation and a challenge: what assumptions have you built your understanding of embodiment and disability upon, and how willing are you to do the difficult work of learning a new grammar of illness, a different way of healing?

DECLAN GOULD

Declan Gould: In the notes section of *The Empty Form Goes All the Way to Heaven*, you write that "the poems in this manuscript extensively use borrowed language" and that "the titles of these poems are drawn from Agnes Martin's *Writings*, except where they are titled after the media and measurement of an individual drawing or painting." What does it mean to write about chronic illness in such a citational way? In other words, for you what is the relationship between chronic illness and using source texts—for example, do you see them as a way to include multiple voices, or as a way of getting out of either/or thinking when it comes to this subject?

Brian Teare: This is a great question. I found undiagnosed illness to be both wordlessly corporeal and hyper-discursive, a paradox the poems often try to enact. For many years, my sense of self was often subsumed by chronic pain, cognitive fog, and other symptoms, and yet, as a patient, I was constantly called upon by Western allopathic medicine to narrate myself. And so I became acutely aware that my sense of self often retreated from the linguistic to the corporeal because of the repeated failure of language to hold or describe my embodied experience. Often I was simply tired of using language at all, given its failure to elicit help from doctors or loved ones. And yet I repeatedly sought medicalization through diagnosis and treatment because I believed my suffering would end if we could just find the right words to describe my illness.

From deep inside the somatic experience of illness, I could at all times feel and hear language flowing through and around me. So when I write, late in the book, "illness means a lot less / self which isn't so bad," I mean that at some point, I started tracking the phrases that passed through the place where I located my sense of self. I started thinking that illness had made me so porous that whatever I was reading or looking at began to feel like "self" or like part of the self, even if only briefly. For a time, illness made me a space language drifts through—each poem a curated arrangement of drift on the gridded page. Of course—as another late poem points out—I found the experience of chronic illness, and chronic pain in particular, to have "a limited vocabulary," but within it, I found another paradox: "the inexhaustible / nature of limitation."

DG: In the text, dwelling in the present tense and in a state of "inbetweenity" (to borrow a term from Brenda Jo Brueggemann) sometimes seems like an impasse imposed by forces beyond your control (such as pain), and at other times seems deliberately cultivated, even aspired-to. So can you talk about suspension—of time, legibility, psychic and somatic states—in *The Empty Form*?

BT: Thank you for your attention to this aspect of the book. I published an early version of some of these poems in a chapbook called *Helplessness* (Goodmorning Menagerie, 2012). The epigraph to that chapbook was drawn, of course, from Agnes Martin, from her essay "On the Perfection Underlying Life": "But helplessness, when fear and dread have run their course, as all passions do, is "the most rewarding state of all." In the context of a long illness, I found this a remarkably provocative argument, and I found her characterization of helplessness as "the most rewarding" state to be a challenge to my own experience of it.

Though I argue with Martin throughout the book, I intend argument as a sign of respect: I take her seriously, even at her most outrageous. In the instance of the above statement, it shocked me to think of helplessness as rewarding. But you're right that she challenged me to think of it as something to which I might cultivate a different relationship, whether I interpret helplessness as my own material circumstances or the more metaphysical situation she intended. Which is another way of saying that much of this book records my coming to terms with an illness that was often disabling, and integrating helplessness into my sense of self was a part of that reckoning.

The multiple aspects of suspension you mention—of time, of legibility, of psyche, of somatic states—are meant, I think, to elicit an experience of helplessness in the reader. Most readers unconsciously expect texts to be like able bodies—legible, unified, meaningful in predictable ways—and I wanted to frustrate that unconscious expectation in poems about disability. I liked the anxiety that early drafts of the poems elicited in some readers: the poem that claims "I don't know / how to read this" indeed quotes one of those readers. When they responded that way, it felt like lipsynch, that they were simply miming what most doctors had said to me about my body, what I had said to myself about my own condition.

Which is to say: I felt the poems had done their job! Having to face choosing how to navigate most of the poems means that a reader pauses at the threshold of meaning before interpreting the text. That pause before making meaning is perhaps the most important moment of suspension in the book, "the most rewarding state" (ha!), though it is of course also often frustrating or painful. In the end, I hope the self-consciousness of not knowing how to proceed makes a reader aware that chronic illness and disability frequently demand a long and profound confrontation with not knowing, a confrontation that permanently changes what it means to know.

DG: Robert McRuer and Alison Kafer (among others) have done a lot of interesting work on queer/crip intersectionality, and certainly your book *Pleasure* and your teaching show your interest in queer theory and queer community. Do you think this background makes its way into *The Empty Form*, or may have in any way primed or prepared you to write about chronic illness and disability?

BT: I wish I could say that I thought about this kind of intersectional politics during the composition of the book. Frankly, I was so overwhelmed with the details of daily life and with the experience of being ill, low-income, and uninsured that intersectionality of this sort, which would no doubt have brought great insight, comfort, and agency, was entirely beyond me. This early isolation meant I didn't know an-often-disabling illness could be included in disability frameworks—maybe

I was too immiserated by medical schemas in which pre-existing medical conditions blocked access! So it took me a while to think of my experience in relation to disability, which, it turned out, is a discourse and a community both inclusive and also always contested and in process. Ultimately I found deep identification with critiques of the medical model of disability—with its assimilationist emphasis on mediation by Western medicine, diagnosis, management, and even "cure"—and kinship with feminist, queer, and "crip" models based on identification, solidarity, community pride, and intersectional analysis.

Now I've begun to think about the ways in which a more Foucauldian reading of illness would highlight both its dependence on medicalization and a resulting hyper-discursivity. This reading would also highlight the way in which repeated medical testing attempts to elicit a "confession" of illness from the body. In Western allopathic medicine, only through testing can the body truly "speak," and then receive diagnosis and treatment—and only testing and diagnosis authenticate the body's confession as "true." Of course, this legitimization is totally dependent on having access to medical care, which, during the time I was most ill, was also largely dependent on being able to get health insurance. For a long time this entire paradigm meant that, according to Western allopathic medicine, I wasn't "really" ill, no matter my history of symptoms, no matter what I said.

Over the years, I've thought a lot about how this system failed and often continues to fail me, how my body refused to confess to doctor after doctor, to test after test. I've thought a lot about how other medical modalities (such as Chinese medicine and osteopathy) see symptom as confession enough, and read the body not through medical testing but through other, less invasive means: educated touch, for instance, the deliberate palpation of pulses or of fascia and other connective tissues. I've thought a lot about how these alternative modalities felt and continue to feel a thousand times more like care than anything I've ever experienced in the disembodied hands of Western allopathic medicine. I've valued Chinese medicine and osteopathy as nonviolent alternatives to a medicalization I ultimately experience as a profound and disturbing violence, a violence that impacts everyone differently depending on their positionality, and targets women, trans, and BIPOC folx especially with unequitable and deadly force.

DG: I've been thinking a lot about what your book might suggest about the concept of disability as a material, embodied constraint that often makes writing more difficult but that might also leads to the creation of new forms. And I like the term "constraint" because it frames the form that the writing takes as the author's way of mediating illness, rather than as a pathological symptom. What are your thoughts on these ways of framing disability writing, and how they might map onto your book?

BT: I like the way you're thinking about disability and illness as contextual "constraints" that inform the act of writing as well as suggest the forms writing might take. By utilizing the "grid" inherent in the digitally typeset page and hanging stanzas in varying proximity to one another within that grid, I hoped that illness would become both more visible and more palpable to readers as they navigated stanzas and their multiple relationships to one another. At other times, by highlighting the intrinsically gridded nature of the sonnet form, I wanted to bring forward the ways lyric traditionally makes claims to a body of meaning adamantly unified by the formal and historical norms of the genre. In experimenting with the grid in these ways, I was curious a) if content and form could share the burden of making disability "visible," and b) if I could sometimes shift the burden of making disability "visible" away from linear narrative and onto poetic form.

As I've suggested, this kind of shifting mimics my experience of reading my own illness and disability: at times my body seems legible, and at other times it resists being read. While I was writing *The Empty Form*, being in physical pain was far more legible to me than the cognitive effects of disorientation, memory loss, and fogginess; persistent physical symptoms like headache and nausea invariably elicited diagnostic language from doctors, whereas more ephemeral and purely subjective symptoms did not. Over time I became interested in the unpredictable quality of where I found limitation to reside—now language, now my body, now Western medical care, now poetry, now my mind. I wanted the book to push against the limitations they all offered.

I also like the word "constraint" because it suggests the material ways that illness and disability literally shape writing as a practice that is as much physical as mental. For me, as a writer coming to chronic illness and disability in my 30s, I was hugely aware of how my writing practice shifted in response—gone were the poems written on foot, gone were the hours and hours immersed in drafting, gone were long poems with long lines. During the worst of it, I wasn't hiking, I had limited cognitive clarity, and I had no stamina—windows of mental acuity and physical energy were unpredictable and short, and so, lying on my side or sitting up in bed, I began to accrue fragments in a file on my laptop. After a while, I began to use phrases from Martin's *Writings* as titles under whose aegis those fragments began to relate to one another in fruitful ways. On days I had fewer cognitive symptoms, I might sit up in a chair and work on one of the ekphrastic sonnets that punctuate the book, Agnes Martin monograph open to a grid into which I'd stare as I worked my way through the mirroring grid of the sonnet.

DG: This is really just a continuation of the previous question, but do you think one of the functions of the grid in *The Empty Form* might be that it enables you to write while ill (in the sense that it provides a scaffolding, form, container, and/or way of holding the various pieces together)? In other words, along with providing a space for curation, a way to suspend meaning-making, pain relief (or at least understanding), and an intimate, sustained engagement with Martin, might the grid also be a useful method for writing under the material constraints of being in chronic, severe pain, foggy-headed, and nauseous? What would you say is the relationship between the grid form and the material, embodied experience of writing while ill?

BT : Absolutely. During the years of writing *The Empty Form*, the grid served as a scaffolding that held me up in ways as much conceptual as they were practical. On the one hand, the grid as I conceived it provides an alternative to Olson's "Projective Verse": the grid focuses not on the line spun out from the poet's breath, the line articulated syllable by syllable by the poet's ear, but rather emphasizes the digitally typeset page as an ocular whole. To conceive of composition-by-page, to conceive of the poem as a grid, shifts the emphasis of poiesis from the poet's breath and ear to the poet's eye, likewise shifting the compositional emphasis from syllable and line to the page entire, thus freeing the lines from a necessarily organic relation to one another. This is not to say that the individual lines in *The Empty Form* don't proceed by breath, by syllable, but that each poem as a whole is no longer formed by the necessity of being through-composed. Because my previous work had been so resolutely Olsonian and so dedicated to the "open field" of writing en plein air, I needed a way to rethink poetic form that could embody the continuous discontinuity of illness and disability as I experienced it. I enjoyed the paradox that this new form of embodiment is less about the ear and more about the eye, a part of the body we think of as more cerebral than visceral.

On the other hand, as you've suggested, the grid allowed for a writing practice literally constrained by illness and disability. The grid could accommodate uncertainty, silence, and contingency more fully than my previous "projective" practice, and it also accommodated long gaps of inactivity. I could hang a few lines or stanzas on the page and come back to them days or weeks later, whereas my previous poems had all been built through nearly continuous work whose integrity depended on an almost uninterrupted process of composition. From the open field to the sickbed, to whole days of writing to a few hours of it: this was a huge shift, and it made me incredibly uncomfortable. At first, the poems of *The Empty Form* didn't even seem like poems because the process of making them was so different. But it didn't take me long to understand that the contingent quality of the stanza arrangements could make meaning—and refuse to make meaning—in ways my previous poems never could.

D G : With this question, I'm thinking about the moments in the book where you point towards the problematics of Christian discourses about suffering as a way into heaven ("Book I of *De Imitatione Christi* says / it is good for man to suffer"), the problematics of Martin's investments in purity ("her core beliefs in inspiration, perfection," and "nonattachment"), and the limitations of Buddhist investments in the empty, clear mind ("I love the teacher Buddha / then the illness worsens // I vomit and weep until empty / he is wrong..."). That being said, how would you say that emptiness signifies in your book? Would it be way off to read the title's references to emptiness and heaven as slightly tongue-in-cheek?

B T : This is potent commentary. It points to the question I eventually found to be at the "heart" of the book: is there a correct form of suffering?

For the person in chronic pain, it seems like a stupid thing to ask, but in the Christian faith with which I was raised, it is a central question whose answer is a forceful YES. Christ is held up as a model all believers should strive to imitate: he first suffers being incarnated as flesh, and then, most famously, he suffers betrayal, persecution, crucifixion, and death, all for the benefit of others. It's not for nothing that *patient*, of medieval origin, derives from the Old French *pacient*, which means "enduring without complaint."

Of course, various forms of Buddhism offer their own compelling and competing readings of suffering. In the theology with which I'm most familiar, the four noble truths center on acknowledging suffering's omnipresence in our lives and its rootedness in our attachment to the experiences of reality offered by our minds and bodies. Suggesting that our minds both hinder our ability to experience the real and offer a way out of delusion, such Buddhism argues that relinquishing our attachments leads to a cessation of suffering.

Ironically, I found that being ill in the context of the West encouraged a much greater attachment to the very body that troubled me. Working together, Western medicine and I treated my body as a sign to which we needed to attach signification—if only we found a diagnosis, my body would be a legible sign, and my suffering would achieve a kind of narrative shape with its attendant proscribed meaning. For a long time I longed for such legibility, and so I scrutinized my bodily experience as best I could, suffering its illegibility all the while suffering the very experiences I hoped would soon cohere into meaning.

All of which is to say that *The Empty Form* is interested—like Agnes Martin was—in the metaphysics of suffering. Of course the poems outright reject Christian readings of suffering, and especially the Christian definition of "patient," though it was useful to understand that such readings and definitions informed and even structured my early experiences of illness. And though poems later in the book often struggle to internalize Buddhist—specifically Zen—readings of suffering, it is Zen that ultimately offered a powerful counter to medical narratives of illness and disability.

For several of the years during which I wrote the book, my care consisted only of zazen, Chinese medicine, and acupuncture. Western allopathic medicine failed me as a low-income, uninsured patient. Eastern practices and healing modalities eventually allowed me to see that my attachment to diagnosis and to the question "Is there a correct form of suffering?" only made my suffering worse. So as I put the book together, I strongly wanted to avoid certain narrative tropes that in the West tend to structure stories about illness and disability. I particularly wanted to avoid the implicitly Christian "redemption" story that narratives of illness often provide—an inkling of which inheres in the colloquialism, "I fell ill," which suggests one must be "saved" by medicine from the original sin of having a body subject to ill health. As in religious narrative where the institution of the Church saves the sinful, medical narrative tends to invest the institution of medicine with the power to save the fallen.

I also wanted to avoid a "pearls of wisdom I learned from my disability" kind of text, the likes of which often treat disability like a foreign culture to be visited and the disabled person like a visionary whose knowledge of the body can be appropriated and used by the able-bodied. Instead, the book offers the narrative of someone trying to suffer his chronic illness correctly, someone who comes late to the realization that just simply suffering will suffice—no need to add the agony of trying to do it right. This insight is what the book's final poem documents: the moment of real happiness that resulted from giving up Christian narratives of illness, suffering, diagnosis, and recovery. There was indeed dear relief and ecstatic clarity in that moment when I realized

> it took a long time   to arrive at being ill

> without falling   I'm happy   I really like

> this painting   there's no salvation in it

So yes, you're right, the book rejects the Christian salvation narratives that many traditional medical narratives offer. But though Zen precepts underlie both Martin's and my own thinking, *The Empty Form* achieves Buddhist nonattachment only to certain concepts and narratives while remaining thoroughly attached to others. Though that has a lot to do with my own limitations as a Western practitioner of meditation and as a latecomer to Buddhist thought, I think it also has a lot to do with my continued attachment to identity politics and to both proprioception and phenomenology—the rootedness in bodily experience and body politics that informs all my writing. I can't imagine emptiness without it filling up with flesh.

DG: Last summer, you told me that you were thinking a lot about the concept of access when you were writing this book. Can you say more about what you mean by access, why it's important to *The Empty Form*, and how you've been thinking about this idea lately (perhaps even for current or future writing projects)?

BT : "Accessibility" means something very different in disability politics and in poetry criticism, but access has been pretty crucial to both discourses, and I'm interested in the ways that the term suggests overlaps between them. Disability literature has long had, like most literatures that emerge from movement politics, a more or less implicit commitment to aesthetic accessibility—to what Amiri Baraka would call, in the context of the Black Arts Movement, "mass art." I came of age as a queer poet during the AIDS epidemic, and so I get this; I was raised on the similarly transparent aesthetics of Gay Liberation and AIDS poetry, both of which aimed to build coalition, document history, protest injustice, mourn our losses, and raise consciousness.

Within the context of disability literature, however, the aesthetic accessibility of "mass art" takes on the additional valence of literal physical accessibility. It's a moral and political good to aesthetically enact the legal demands of the ADA in whatever ways one can, and in writing *The Empty Form*, I was often acutely aware of seeming to fail to do so. However, thanks to feminist and queer theory and my communities, I have also long been wary of the hegemonic potential of any ideology, including that of mass art, whose poetics can be prescriptive and restrictive concerning a poem's behavior and appearance. By revisiting the conceptual parameters of how poems behave and appear on the page, I wanted to question what I sometimes perceive to be ableist norms of literacy and of meaning-making that persist even in disability poetry.

In asking readers to navigate the different arrangement of each page, by putting readers in a position of "helplessness" when it comes to meaning-making, I'm asking them to interrogate their assumptions about how the body of a poem achieves legibility. How does a poem on the page even register to readers as a poem? As we know, it's by behaving predictably, like the majority of poems we've been trained to read: left-justified lines moving down the page in a narratively and grammatically linear manner, their hypotactical construction adhering to the dictates of rational and logical thought. But if our bodies and minds can't always "behave" according to social norms, why should our poems? I think this is a useful line of questioning.

Throughout this interview, I've been talking as though the poems were deliberate acts of will, conceptual objects I deployed with full self-awareness. However, I want to stress that the theorizing I've been doing here arose from writing the poems themselves, which in turn arose from the conditions of my own embodied life. Writing was entirely improvisational and contingent, dependent on my own fluctuating health and ability. The poetics did not precede the poems' forms and behaviors, but rather emerged as a description of how the poems were made and the often unarticulated concepts that guided the making.

And though I can be critical of the sometimes normalizing formal imperatives of "mass art," I want to stress that the book is not a critique of such accessibility and the important political work it does. I believe in the power of literature to build coalition, document history, protest injustice, mourn our losses, and raise consciousness. I would suggest, though, that *The Empty Form* offers a formal experiment that embodies and enacts physical and cognitive difference, and that experimental poetics can articulate and bear witness to political life in new and useful ways.

DG: *The Empty Form* takes place during a time of crisis, outside of but also before diagnosis. Do you have plans to write about the next stage (e.g. living with illness post-diagnosis or post-crisis, when [self-]care may be oriented towards maintenance rather than rehabilitation)? More broadly speaking, what direction has your poetry taken since *The Empty Form*?

BT (in 2022): Given that my poetics tends to arise from the act of writing poetry, and that my theorizing is mostly a pragmatist act of relating thought and writing back to the context of their emergence from an embodied life, it should come as no surprise that I don't (can't!) really anticipate my books. In the same way I didn't expect to write about illness and disability, after finishing *The Empty Form*, I had no plans to write further about illness or the politics and pragmatics of living with and caring for multiple chronic conditions.

I worked on *The Empty Form* off and on from the summer of 2009 to January of 2015. After that I entered a year of total silence in terms of poetry, a year during which I concentrated on teaching, reading, and healing in the wake of helpful diagnostic care from a holistic medical doctor. When poems began to return in 2016, it felt like I had to relearn how to write. My sense of scale and duration had gotten so calibrated to a bodymind constrained by crisis, I didn't know how to inhabit a proprioceptive field that was different from those of both pre-illness and acute illness. "for five years / my ill body killed me / while it kept me alive," I write in "Sitting River Meditation"; the first question to emerge out of that silence was "Who am I / now."

The book that answers that question did continue some of the ecopoetic practices of *Companion Grasses*: writing on foot in the field, integrating embodied perception and research into natural history and environmental politics. For the first two-thirds of the book, I largely reworked abandoned drafts and years of notebook entries written on the hoof, writing that glossed over the fact that I was sick. I'd written them during hours I was well enough to be out and about, during years I couldn't sustain the energy to finish anything long. So in "Toxics Release Inventory" and in most of the newest poems, I kept in mind arguments made by Kafer and Sarah Jaquette Ray, and tried to work against environmental writing that renders the body of the naturalist/observer entirely transparent, a transparency that both reifies mind-body dualism and implicitly renders the "naturalist" able-bodied and healthy in a way that mirrors old school ideologies that equate nature with health and reject illness as unnatural and somehow "degenerate." Ironically, I'd written the final poems in *Companion Grasses* during the onset of chronic illness, but you'd never know it—so this is a tendency of which my own work's been guilty.

And though the poems of *Doomstead Days* depend on the figure of the walker—a Thoreauvian saunterer and urban flâneur—the latter third of the book explicitly records a shift in this figure, who acknowledges the constraint of chronic pain as well as physical vulnerability. The two "sitting meditations" are part of this shift, as are "Olivine, Quartz, Granite, Carnelian" and the title poem, which in part documents a life-changing osteopathic manual manipulation treatment that both rid me of occipital migraines and released the poem. I'd argue that *Doomstead Days* as a whole points to some of the overlaps between ecological thought and what Kafer calls a political/relational model of disability, particularly in its vision of embodiment as contextual, networked, porous, deeply precarious, and full of pleasure. "Eveything's body / connected by this / totally elastic / materiality," I write, "I feel as ecstatic / wide dilation." But the book also acknowledges this materiality as "awkward, okay" (to say the least!), given that the ecstatic connection is also polluted and polluting, full of toxins that flow both ways. In writing that final poem, I found that ecological, queer, feminist, and disability critiques dovetailed in their rejection of the violent patriarchal fantasy represented by the doomstead: to wall the body off from the world, "as if there were / ever a way to stay / safely-self-contained."

DG: In their keynote address at the 2018 New Disability Poetics Symposium, "How I Said It With My Hands: Rejecting Reasonable Accommodation," Meg Day drew a clear line between disability poetics and crip poetics. Day defines disability poetics as an essentially assimilationist discourse: "it's a name, a label, a way for disabled poets & therefore disability poetics to flag the moments in which our bodies & lives are co-opted & used without our consent, but never included on our own terms." In contrast, they call for a "crip poetics" that is written by and for crip poets and centers not institutions, but self-determined discourse: "How could I advocate for a poetics that keeps disability only when it is reasonable; only as an occasional addition, a tokenized afterthought." How would you describe your understanding of disability poetics versus crip poetics, and how do you think *The Empty Form Goes All the Way to Heaven* relates to this binary?

BT : Meg's keynote hit the room with tremendous emotional, ethical, and intellectual force. I remember the affective experience of it well, grounded as it was in their vulnerability, trust, vital anger, and rigorous argumentation. The line they drew between disability and crip poetics was new to me then, as was the rhetorical gesture of addressing the nondisabled in the audience directly—"This talk is not for you. It is for my kin. You are witnessing the credo—nothing about us without us—in rare and real time"—and these moves remain for me incredibly generative. I continue to think with and through and alongside them, and like any system partly built on an us/them binary, it can generate critical self-questioning in those of us whose bodies, life experiences, identities, and poetries don't always fall neatly into an either/or situation.

As I've already suggested, when I began writing *The Empty Form*, I didn't have much exposure to disability or crip poetics, and certainly hadn't read the theorists (Clare, Kafer, Kuppers, McRuer, Ray, Siebers, etc.) that have become so important to me in the years since, thanks in part to your recommendations. Though I'd been sick off and on since I was a teenager, chronic illness, sustained periods of disability, and the pain of medicalization and medical debt permanently entered my life in 2009. Somehow, not long after that, the editors of *Beauty Is a Verb* heard that I was writing new work about that experience. Their generous invitation to submit and their acceptance of early drafts of poems from *The Empty Form* really moved me, and also made me begin to question how—and with whom—I identify.

In the years since, I've come to understand that critical self-questioning—rooted now in having permanent invisible disabilities and the privilege of medication, diet, and physical therapies that often allow me to pass as able-bodied—is an important part of chronic illness, pain, and fluctuating ability. I know my own experience, and remain accountable to the many ways it does not parallel the experiences of other crip- and disability-identified folx. Kafer's sense of "crip" in *Feminist Queer Crip* resonates with Meg's: it is more "contestatory" than a disability politics because it is "more willing to explore the potential risks and exclusions of identity politics." At the same time, Kafer argues that "crip" as a term contains a kind of "potential expansiveness" and "flexibility" when it comes to inclusion. Reading her essay "After Crip, Crip Afters" in the Crip Temporalities issue of *South Atlantic Quarterly*, I deeply identify with her sense of "crip" as an attachment: "Attachment as affiliation, as relationality, as solidarity."

When I first began writing *The Empty Form*, such feelings of affiliation, relationality, and solidarity largely lay in the future. My experience of being an acutely ill, low-income, uninsured adjunct in San Francisco was, as I've said, hugely isolating, in large part because it was a period of deep uncertainty, lack of care, exploitative labor, and struggle on many fronts. That period of time happened to coincide with Eleni Stecopolous's curated series "The Poetics of Healing," which I was ironically never well enough to attend. But there were also related Nonsite Collective events, a few of which I could attend because they were within walking distance of Albion Street, and one of those events introduced me to David Wolach and their work.

It mattered to me and to the writing of *The Empty Form* that folks like Eleni and Petra Kuppers and Bhanu Kapil were writing texts and creating performances so focused on embodiment, bodywork, and poetics. David Wolach's critiques of medicalization would become hugely helpful in processing my own disappointing and wounding experiences with Western allopathic medicine. I felt they were my "people," even if they largely didn't know who I was. I kept their writing close. I still think through and alongside Eleni's *Armies of Compassion* and *Visceral Poetics* and also David Wolach's *Hospitalogy* and all of Bhanu's books. I believe Amber DiPietra's and Denise Leto's amazing collaboration *Waveform* came out of this time period as well, and I think of Hilary Gravendyk's *harm* and her crucial article on Eigner, "Chronic Poetics," as late products of this discourse community too.

I suspect I found their focus on embodiment, healing, and the experience of medicalization so welcoming and generative because their focus wasn't on identity per se. I didn't experience any conflict around invisible disability, which at that point of nascency—when I didn't quite know what was happening to me or who I was or how I identified or what *The Empty Form* would even become—was crucial. To be in relation without much actual sociality was just right at that moment in time. So in retrospect I'd say my affiliation and feelings of solidarity began with events I was not well enough to attend!

Those feelings later extended more broadly, thanks to the generosity of Jennifer Bartlett, Sheila Black, and Michael Northen and the poets of *Beauty Is a Verb*. And when I was finally able to attend a somatics-centered event led by Eleni and Petra—at the Ecopoetics Conference in 2013—it was a powerful moment of coming full circle, moving with them in space and time at last! The poem "The process called destiny in which we are the material to be dissolved" was written after that event, and contains a useful idea of Eleni's: a therapeutic form of impasse. It helped me at that time when I was still undiagnosed and receiving forms of holistic health care that sustained and healed but could not "cure" me.

DG: Rather than making an argument, presenting a conventional narrative, or providing hard and fast answers, *The Empty Form* seems to reframe the subjects at hand, asking generative questions and offering innovative ways of thinking and writing about topics such as pain, chronic illness, disability, and healing. What new questions, angles, and/or modes of thinking do you think allopathic medicine and medical professionals might gain access to by reading works of "embodiment and bodywork" poetics like *The Empty Form*?

BT: This is such a good, provocative question. As I've said, I started writing the book without much context or support for my experiences of illness and disability. Inspired by Agnes Martin's grids and Ch'an and Zen Buddhist writing, I built poems that felt like they could hold the psychic and somatic traces of illness and resulting disability in all their instability, ephemerality, and precarity. I stayed true to that practice even as I became more informed by writers, thinkers, activists, bodyworkers, Chinese medical practitioners, and zazen. As you've suggested, *The Empty Form* contrasts strongly with conventional works of narrative medicine. It is nonnarrative, it is skeptical of what Eli Clare calls "the medical-industrial complex," and it resists being instrumentalized in obvious ways. And through recent dialogues with doctors, medical residents, caregivers, and scholars in medical humanities, I've come to see that these might in fact be the primary strengths of the book, as discomfiting and frustrating to readers as these qualities can be.

Medical knowledge is a form of literacy that has close structural kinship to narrative literacy—both are linear, emphasize cause and effect, thrive off categorization, and seek denouements that resolve (and sometimes also absolve) conflict. There are real rewards to writing narratively and good reasons to do so, particularly in terms of the politics of accessibility we've already talked about. And though representational aesthetics has a politics I respect, I find myself ambivalent anyway. My ambivalence is about the relationship of aesthetics to institutional power, and perhaps echoes Meg's ambivalence about disability poetics. We can't entirely control with whom and with what we collude when we offer representations of ourselves. And given that so much of my physical and psychic suffering was amplified by the failure of Western allopathic medicine to "read" my body correctly and offer meaningful care, it would be both a falsehood and a betrayal of that experience to absolve readers of the same conflict.

But when I write non-narratively, when I offer poems whose visuality challenges conventional notions of "the poem," when I critique Western allopathic medicine, I court all kinds of other risks, the largest one being inaccessibility. I want to push against the notion that perceived aesthetic inaccessibility is in any way a barrier equivalent to the structural inaccessibility of a bathroom or a lecture hall. As an educator, I'm highly aware that perceived inaccessibility stems in large part from the narrowness of literacy in the US. Even college students who specialize in literature aren't often taught to read and appreciate poems that move differently than first-person, left-justified poems in regular stanza forms—thus they can't account for poems that move through disjunction, dysfluency, and visual difference. Of course, these students might have the time and the inclination to attempt to gain the literacies to do so. But what about medical students, whose humanities educations likely don't extend past general education requirements?

I don't know how to intervene on a large scale in medical education, or how to create the necessary buy-in from medical educators and students, or how to convince skeptical medical humanists that narrative can be damagingly hegemonic, but my fantasy is that acquiring more capacious textual literacies could prepare doctors and caregivers to respond to and hold with mindful care a wider variety of patients, patient testimonies, and patient experiences of the institution of medicine. My fantasy is that such literacies would also decenter narrative and linguistic fluency from the privileged position they hold in medical humanities. Sadly, accounts of disability and illness are often deemed valuable to the institution of medicine only when they are narrative and when they embody ableist fictions of fluency. I'd love to see models of medical literacy that encompass fragments, stutters, gaps, repetitions, interruptions, irruptions, and dysfluencies not as flaws but as important indicators of experiences rich in signification. I'd love to see models of medical literacy that approach apparent linguistic difficulty and perceived inaccessibility as equally important and rich invitations to collaborate on making meaning together.

DG: Rereading *The Empty Form* and the first version of our interview now, two plus years into the COVID-19 pandemic, many of the ideas that they investigate strike me as very timely and "universal." After all, the pandemic has foregrounded our vulnerability and interdependence, confronted many nondisabled people with the uncertainty and contingency of our existence, highlighted the limitations of (and inequitable access to) Western medicine, and raised questions about what illness can reveal about ourselves and our social, structural, and discursive norms. How has the pandemic changed your relationship with or understanding of these poems, and what do you think it means to reissue these poems at this point in the COVID era?

B T : My gut response is: too much hasn't changed. Neoliberal capitalism remains an intractable life-threatening preexisting condition, affecting citizens unequally across lines of class, race, gender, and ability. Access to vaccines, antiviral treatments, and PPE has often followed those patterns, though it has fluctuated so wildly across the past two plus years that it's hard to generalize with any precision. Early on in the pandemic, though, with Trump in charge of misinformation and the CDC falling apart, I felt the eerie certainty I first felt when I was young and AIDS was a death sentence: government oligarchs really do want us to die, they really don't care, nothing matters to them but profit and power. Teaching via Zoom late that spring, I thought about who had no choice about taking health risks when showing up to work; a few of my friends in Philly got sick right away from their workplaces, though they luckily recovered. All of which is to say that I wonder for whom the pandemic has truly brought home "vulnerability and interdependence"? I suppose the skeptic in me believes that COVID has, like our political system and like climate crisis, largely done the opposite: citizens who were already vulnerable feel even more so (that is, if they are still alive), and citizens who have had the lifelong privilege to deny interdependence have gotten violently protective of that fiction.

The idealist in me: where is he? I suppose he's writing this answer now, looking forward to the reissue of this book in six months! I suppose my idealist also wrote these poems with the belief that there was value in documenting (however oblique the document) what my friend Miranda Mellis called at the time a "healing crisis." I reread these poems now and I'm grateful to have a document of the extreme debility, confusion, and anxiety of those years; I'm grateful to have a document of low income, disability, and illness before the Affordable Care Act, as flawed as that legislation is; I'm grateful to have a document that testifies to the power of holistic modalities of medical care; I'm grateful to have a document that returns me to Agnes Martin's art and writing without undue pressure on it to "save" me; I'm grateful to have a document that records, almost in real time, my coming to an understanding with my own suffering. It was important to understand that suffering not only as individual, as a physical and metaphysical experience, but also as contextual, the direct result of disenfranchising economic and legal policies. Why might that kind of document be meaningful or useful to others right now? I suppose both my skeptic and my idealist believe we—and here I intend the largest possible "we," inclusive of all human and more-than-human beings—are in a global healing crisis, outcome uncertain.

2017/2022

Acknowledgments

Many thanks to the editors in whose ventures these poems have previously appeared, sometimes in much earlier versions :

Academy of American Poets: "*Perceiving* is the same as *receiving* and it is the same as *responding*"; *Apiary Magazine*: "There are two endless directions. In and out," "I pretend I was looking at the blank page," and "We seem to be winning and losing, but there is no losing"; *Beauty is a Verb: The New Poetry of Disability*: "Then I painted the two rectangles," "There are two endless directions. In and out," "With these rectangles I didn't know at the time exactly why," and "The writing fills the space as drawing would"; *Chicago Review*: "*Defeated* you will stand at the door of your house and welcome the unknown," "With these rectangles I didn't know at the time exactly why," "This poem, like the paintings, is not really about nature," "*Defeated*, you will perhaps go a little bit further," and "Look between the rain. The drops are insular"; *Cultural Society*: "Going on where hope and desire have been left behind is a discipline," and "This developing awareness I will also call 'the work.' It is a most important part of the work"; *Denver Quarterly*: "I lay down my gaze as one lay's down one's weapon," "The writing fills the space as drawing would," and "When I cover the square surface with rectangles, it destroys its power"; *eleveneleven*: "The process called destiny in which we are the material to be dissolved," and "When you come to the end of all ideas you will still have no definitive knowledge on the subject." *Journal of Medical Humanities*: "I give up facts entirely," "There is the work in our minds, the work in our hands, and the work as a result," "We seem to be winning and losing, but there is no losing," "When pride in some form is lost, we feel very different," and "With a soft attitude, you receive more"; *The Offending Adam*: "And to think I am small and the work is small," "Like a dignified journey with no trouble and no goal on and on," "There are an infinite number of different kinds of happiness," and "watercolor and graphite on paper, fifteen by fifteen inches"; *Oversound*: "I am going to work in order to see myself and free myself," "I want to repeat: there are no valid thoughts about art," "One must see the ideal in one's own mind. It is like the memory of perfection," and "We are not the instruments of fate nor are we the pawns of fate we are the material of fate"; *A Public Space*: "If you don't like chaos, you're a classicist" and "If you like it, you're a romantic"; *SET*: "Neither objects nor space, not time, not anything—no forms," "I'm not trying to describe anything. I'm looking for the perfect space," "Not to know, but to go on," and "I am nothing absolutely. There is this other thing going on"; *VOLT*: "pencil on aquatint ground, twelve and a half by twelve inches" and "watercolor, ink and gouache on paper, nine and a quarter by nine and a quarter inches"; *Wordgathering:* "If there is a bare spot on the ground the best possible weed for that environment will grow," "Somebody's got to sit down and really want it," and "We think that at last our feet are on the right path and we will not falter or fail."

Jennifer Bartlett, Sheila Black, and Michael Northen generously first gave me a place to write and think about the interplay between illness, disability, poetry, and spirituality.

Genna Kohlhardt and Julie Strand at Goodmorning Menagerie first gathered many of these poems in the limited edition chapbook, *Helplessness*.

Genine Lentine first offered herself as a compassionate interlocutor whose reading clarified the direction this book eventually took.

Without the companionable critical intelligences of Gillian Conoley and Rick Barot, both of whom offered generous editorial guidance, this book would not have found its final form.

And without Janet Holmes, this book would not have found *this* form at all.

Thank you to all who helped guide these poems.

I owe particular thanks to all the healers—particularly Marintha Tewksbury, Antje Hofmeister, Eva Zeller, and Dr. Heidi Wittels—who helped guide me in crisis, when no one else could.

And in 2022, I thank Declan Gould. It's been an honor to investigate together what I was after in writing *The Empty Form*, and a lesson in generosity to revisit, revise, and extend our years-long conversation about disability and poetics.

I also thank Dr. Daniel Becker and Dr. Benjamin Martin for the invitation to speak about (non)narrative medicine to the medical residents at UVA Medical Center. And Dr. Martin and Dr. Irène Mathieu for the invitation to visit with their medical humanities students, and for opening and sustaining new lines of dialogue between poetry and medicine, and caregivers and patients.

And to everyone at Nightboat Books who helped realize this reprint and give the book a second life – Stephen Motika, Lindsey Boldt, Gia Gonzales, Kit Schluter, Caelan Nardone, and Lina Bergamini – "grateful" doesn't cover the amplitude of feeling I have for you all.

Notes

The titles of these poems are drawn from Agnes Martin's *Writings*, except where they are titled after the media and measurements of an individual drawing or painting. On a very few occasions the title is taken from a text about Martin's work.

The poems in this manuscript extensively use borrowed language. Such borrowings are rarely indicated in the poems themselves, so let the following archive serve as notice. I apologize in advance for any unintentional omissions.

Baas, Jacquelynn and Mary Jane Jacob, eds. *Buddha Mind in Contemporary Art*. Berkeley: University of California Press, 2004.

Barthes, Roland. *Michelet*. Trans. Richard Howard. New York: Hill and Wang, 1987.

Blanchot, Maurice. *Writing the Disaster*. Trans. Ann Smock. Lincoln: University of Nebraska Press, 1995.

Borden, Lizzie. Letter to Suzanne Delahanty. Undated. TS. University of Pennsylvania Rare Books and Manuscripts Library, Philadelphia.

Cage, John. *Silence: Lectures and Writings*. Hanover: Wesleyan University Press, 1973.

Cage, John and Joan Retallack. *Musicage: Cages Muses on Words, Art, and Music*. Hanover: Wesleyan University Press, 1996.

Chave, Anna C. "Agnes Martin: 'Humility, the Beautiful Daughter . . . All of Her Ways Are Empty.'" *Agnes Martin*. Ed. Barbara Haskell. New York: Whitney Museum of Modern Art, 1992.

Cooke, Lynne, Karen Kelly, and Barbara Schröder, eds. *Agnes Martin*. New York: Dia Art Foundation, 2011.

Damasio, Antonio. *Descartes' Error: Emotion, Reason and the Human Brain*. New York: Avon Books, 1994.

de Zegher, Catherine and Hendel Teicher, eds. *3 X Abstraction: New Methods of Drawing by Hilma af Klint, Emma Kunz and Agnes Martin*. New York: The Drawing Center and Yale University Press, 2005.

DiPietra, Amber and Denise Leto. *Waveform*. Chicago: Kenning Editions, 2011.

Dogen, *Moon in a Dewdrop: Writings of Zen Master Dogen*. Ed. Kazuaki Tanahashi. New York: North Point Press, 1985.
Egan, Charles, Ed. and Trans. *Clouds Thick, Whereabouts Unknown: Poems by Zen Monks of China*. New York: Columbia University Press, 2010.

Eigner, Larry. *The Collected Poems of Larry Eigner*, Volumes 1–4. Curtis Faville and Robert Grenier, eds. Stanford: Stanford University Press, 2010.

Fraser, Kathleen. "Wing." *il cuore: the heart | Selected Poems 1970–1995*. Hanover: Wesleyan University Press, 1997.

Glimcher, Arne. *Agnes Martin: Paintings, Writings, Remembrances*. London and New York: Phaidon Press, 2012.

Grosseteste, Robert. *On Light*. Trans. Clare C. Riedl. Milwaukee: Marquette University Press, 1942.

Guest, Barbara. *The Red Gaze*. Middletown: Wesleyan University Press, 2005.

Hinton, David, ed. and trans. *Classical Chinese Poetry: An Anthology*. New York: Farrar, Straus and Giroux, 2008.

_____. *Hunger Mountain: A Field Guide to Mind and Landscape*. Boston: Shambhala Publications, 2010.

Hirshfield, Jane. *Nine Gates: Entering the Mind of Poetry*. New York: Harper Collins, 1997.

Johnson, Barbara. "Apostrophe, Animation, Abortion." *The Lyric Theory Reader*. Eds. Virginia Jackson and Yopie Prins. Baltimore: Johns Hopkins University, 2014.

Kaptchuk, Ted. J. *The Web That Has No Weaver: Understanding Chinese Medicine*. Chicago: Contemporary Books, 200.

á Kempis, Thomas. *The Imitation of Christ*. Trans. John Payne. New York: Manlius, 1816.

Krauss, Rosalind. "The /Cloud/." *Agnes Martin*. Ed. Barbara Haskell. New York: Whitney Museum of Modern Art, 1992.

_____. "Grids." *The Originality of the Avant-garde and Other Modernist Myths*. Cambridge: MIT Press, 1985.
Kuriyama, Shigehisa. *The Expressiveness of the Body and the Divergence of Greek and Chinese Medicine*. Brooklyn: Zones Books, 1999.

Kyger, Joanne. *Again: Poems 1980-2000*. Albuquerque: La Alameda Press, 2001.

Lao-Tzu. *Taoteching*. Trans. Red Pine. Port Townsend: Copper Canyon Press, 2009.

Laozi. *Daode Jing*. Trans. Thomas Meyer. Chicago: Flood Editions, 2005.

Larson, Kay. *Where the Heart Beats: John Cage, Zen Buddhism, and the Inner Life of Artists*. New York: The Penguin Press, 2012.

Li He. *Goddesses, Ghosts, and Demons: The Collected Poems of Li He*. Trans. J.D. Frodsham. San Francisco: North Point Press, 1983.

Mann, Felix. *The Treatement of Disease by Acupuncture*. London: William Heinemann Medical Books, Ltd., 1967.

Martin, Agnes. *Writings/Schriften*. Ed. by Dieter Schwarz. Ostfildern-Ruit: Hatje Cantz Verlag, 2005.

Mavor, Carol. *Reading Boyishly: Roland Barthes, J. M. Barrie, Jacques Henri Lartigue, Marcel Proust, and D. W. Winnicott*. Durham: Duke University Press, 2008.

Prendeville, Brendan. "The Meanings of Acts: Agnes Martin and the Making of Americans." *Oxford Art Journal*, 31.1 (2008): 51–73.

Red Pine, trans. *Poems of the Masters: China's Classic Anthology of T'and and Sung Dynasty Verse*. Port Townsend: Copper Canyon Press, 2003.

_____. *The Zen Teaching of Bodhidharma*. New York: North Point Press, 1987.

Scarry, Elaine. *The Body in Pain: The Making and Unmaking of the World*. New York: Oxford University Press, 1985.

Sedgwick, Eve Kosofsky. "Making Things, Practicing Emptiness." *The Weather in Proust*. Ed. Jonathan Goldberg. Durham: Duke University Press, 2011.

Stalling, Jonathan. *Poetics of Emptiness: Transformations of Asian Thought in American Poetry*. New York: Fordham University Press, 2010.

Stecopolous, Eleni. *Armies of Compassion*. Long Beach: Palm Press, 2010.

Sze, Arthur. *The Silk Dragon: Translations from the Chinese*. Port Townsend: Copper Canyon Press, 2001.

Tuttle, Richard. "What Does One Look at in an Agnes Martin Painting? Nine Musings on the Occasion of Her Ninetieth Birthday." *American Art*, 16.3 (Autumn, 2002): 92-95.

Wallis, Glenn, trans. *The Dhammapada: Verses on the Way*. New York: Random House, 2004.

Wittgenstein, Ludwig. *The Wittgenstein Reader*. Ed. Anthony Kenny. Oxford: Blackwell Publishers, 1994.

Wolach, David. *Occultations*. No location given: Black Radish Books, 2010.

Yunte Huang. *Shi: A Radical Reading of Chinese Poetry*. New York: Roof Books, 1997.

A 2020 Guggenheim Fellow, Brian Teare is the author of six critically acclaimed books, including *Companion Grasses* and *Doomstead Days*, winner of the Four Quartets Prize, and a finalist for the National Book Critics Circle, Kingsley Tufts, and Lambda Literary Awards. His most recent book is a reissue of *The Empty Form Goes All the Way to Heaven*. After over a decade of teaching and writing in the San Francisco Bay Area, and eight years in Philadelphia, he's now an Associate Professor of Poetry at the University of Virginia. An editorial board member of *Poetry Daily*, he lives in Charlottesville, where he makes books by hand for his micropress, Albion Books.

Nightboat Books

Nightboat Books, a nonprofit organization, seeks to develop audiences for writers whose work resists convention and transcends boundaries. We publish books rich with poignancy, intelligence, and risk. Please visit nightboat.org to learn about our titles and how you can support our future publications.

The following individuals have supported the publication of this book. We thank them for their generosity and commitment to the mission of Nightboat Books:

Kazim Ali
Anonymous (4)
Abraham Avnisan
Jean C. Ballantyne
The Robert C. Brooks Revocable Trust
Amanda Greenberger
Rachel Lithgow
Anne Marie Macari
Elizabeth Madans
Elizabeth Motika
Thomas Shardlow
Benjamin Taylor
Jerrie Whitfield & Richard Motika

This book is made possible, in part, by grants from the New York City Department of Cultural Affairs in partnership with the City Council and the New York State Council on the Arts Literature Program.